Salem
THE LOST BONES

R. CURTIS CHAPIN
AUGUSTA VALLS

Archway Publishing books may be ordered through booksellers or by contacting:

Archway Publishing
1663 Liberty Drive
Bloomington, IN 47403
www.archwaypublishing.com
844-669-3957

Cover Courtesy Design by Bruno L. Sicilia
Interior Image Credit: R. Curtis Chapin

ISBN: 978-1-6657-3868-2 (sc)
ISBN: 978-1-6657-3867-5 (hc)
ISBN: 978-1-6657-3869-9 (e)

Library of Congress Control Number: 2023902867

Print information available on the last page.

Archway Publishing rev. date: 4/17/2023

ARCHWAY
PUBLISHING

A special dedication to my children and grandchildren who
helped me all the way—they are truly amazing.
Special acknowledgment to Lizita, my granddaughter, the computer wizard.
Augusta

FOREWORD

Contrary to what you expect from the title of this book, this one is not about the Salem Witch Trials, as many if not all books that address this topic explain, in detail, the history of those trials. They try to explain how and why the judges accepted the proofs and testimonies of witchcraft and the Devil's presence among the terrified villagers.

This book is the story of Curtis, my husband, and how he unearthed, studied, and identified the remains of the martyrs accused, hanged, and buried in Salem. Their bones were hidden for over three hundred years. Several projects to find them failed. They have rested peacefully in a sacred place.

Forty years passed before he decided to write this book. During those years, new books were written, books that he bought and read. He either agreed or disagreed with their conclusions, but they nevertheless added information to his story.

He collected pages, reports, photographs, descriptions, and small notes by the hundreds. During his last year, we recorded many thoughts, ideas, and deductions that gathered in his mind. He died before finishing this book. I considered it my duty to him to fulfill what kept him motivated until his passing.

He hoped that his book would bring comfort and closure to the descendants of the victims who may have carried shame and doubt about the honesty and integrity of their ancestors for more than three hundred years.

DNA science will help to identify the remains of their family members. The can either keep them in their actual sacred tomb or move them to private cemeteries.

This book is for them.

CONTENTS

CHAPTER 1

Now

My name is Robert Curtis Chapin Jr. I was forty-five years old and living in Lincoln, Massachusetts when, in November 1978, I discovered the remains of the innocent victims hanged in Salem in 1692. At the time, I had three jobs. I was a teacher, an educational specialist for emotionally disturbed children, ages seven to fifteen in the Brookline public school system. In the early afternoon, I worked as a membership director at the Waltham Boys' Club, and I was as a resident overseer of the Codman House, Lincoln, Massachusetts. Part of my job was making an inventory of documents, letters, furniture, decorations, and art objects which belonged to the property dating back to the eighteenth century. I was also rebuilding the Italian garden according to the drawings I found among the documents.

The Codman House was a huge mansion, which once had been the home of the Codman family. The Codman's were shipping merchants, and since 1735, when they built the house, many generations of Codman's lived and worked there until the last survivor died. The inventory and classification of the documents became overwhelming. Finally, I was allowed to retain the assistance of Robert Howie, the archivist of St. Michael's Church, Marblehead, Massachusetts. It was the second Anglican missionary outpost in the Puritan bastion of New England. It was somewhat ironic since one of the major reasons the Puritans emigrated was to establish their own theocracy, free from the domination of the Anglican Church.

The archives relating to church events and activities at St. Michael's Church were surprisingly detailed. They dated back to the original subscription of members prior to the construction in 1714 and 1715. Howie also noted a 1771 entry that recorded a church council decision to seal up the door leading to the church basement.

Howie's examination of the church records revealed that, during the first years of the congregation, ten individuals had been buried beneath the church. Although records clearly stated the number of individuals, their identities, and dates, they did not state the location of the caskets or whether actual brick crypts were constructed. In late 1978, Howie became interested in the Episcopalian practice of interring members of their congregation in sub-church crypts. He started digging under the church to locate the coffins of the ten people buried there. Instead, he found loose bones.

Howie wasn't sure what animal the bones were from, until the day he found several human skulls under the floor of the church. He piled the skulls and other bones in his office and in the corridor. He was both confused and fascinated. That was not the way a church would inter its dead. Either they were buried without the rector's knowledge, or the rector was involved in a secret and unusual act. For an unknown reason, they were not interred according to acceptable religious procedures. He suspected that those were not the ones recorded.

Howie wanted my advice, since I had previous experiences digging into Native American burial sites. I had no free time and had to ignore his pleas. Nevertheless, the human skulls were a mystery. Since St. Michael's was built in 1714, and the entrance to the basement was sealed sixty years later, those bones should have been placed shortly before, and belonged to the colonial era. One day, Howie mentioned that one of the skulls was serrated horizontally. This was the result of a procedure made during an autopsy to examine the brain, a forbidden practice at the time. There was an exception: it was acceptable *if the deceased was a criminal*.

That information triggered my curiosity. Finally, I made the drive to Marblehead. Howie had found eleven skulls and several bones. He arranged the skulls on a bench. I was immediately drawn to one of them. It had been sawed around the circumference of the skull and the entire cranium was severed. My first assessment was that the remains were undoubtedly a secondary burial. There were no coffins. From that first encounter, I saw that all the skulls belonged to adults. None were children. That eliminated the possibility of a sudden, fatal, and highly contagious disease in a small community.

I decided to spend some time investigating those remains. While driving home, an idea came to me like lightning. Struck, I had to stop, move to the shoulder, and think. I knew that the Salem trials and hangings resulted in approximately that same number of victims. I also remembered that the bodies had disappeared. Was it possible somebody reburied them under the church? Why? More than twenty years had passed between their deaths and the building of the church. That would explain the secondary burial. My life turned upside down that day. Immediately, and the next day, I set the necessary steps in motion.

I asked for an appointment with Father George Westerberg, vestry of St. Michael's Church, to obtain his permission to continue Howie's digging. Once I received his letter granting permission, the next project was to prepare a more respectful and secure location for the bones for professional study and classification. The corridor was not the appropriate place. I set up eleven planks supported with sawhorses and arranged them around the big rooms in Codman House. On every plank, I put one skull and numbered it. The one severed in half was number one. I was fascinated with it. I also moved all the other bones.

On my first exploration of the basement, I found the conditions difficult in many ways. The average space was two feet high. The soil was fine dust. A lot of garbage was also buried: mostly whiskey bottles and a collection of rusted tools, nails, wood scraps, and baskets, among other objects. The bones of eleven corpses would mean a lot of careful shifting. I needed several tools to do a professional job. These included respirator masks, small shovels, plastic bags to set aside the soil already shifted, powerful lights, sieves, and an industrial vacuum cleaner with fine filters at the tip of the hose. On top of everything, the excavation had to be done during the night to avoid the neighbor's suspicion. And questions that we were yet not able to answer. At the same time, I read extensively on the Salem Witch trials and all the individuals involved. There began to emerge clues linking St. Michael's Church, Salem Village, Gallows Hill, and the key figures involved in that historical period.

I contacted Stephen Loring, student of archaeology at the University of Massachusetts. On December 26, 1978, we began to excavate the burial pit or ossuary. The archaeological priority was to locate the area beneath the church where the ten recorded burials were located. We wanted, if possible, to identify one or more of the anticipated grave burials to rule out any confusion between the Salem (?) remains and the official church burials. There were physical and logistical problems associated with the entire dig. Access under the church was through a small door under the south portico. This led to a narrow corridor about twenty feet long and ending at a tiny furnace room. The furnace room had been constructed in 1880 to provide coal heat to the church. The furnace room was enlarged slightly in 1942, when heating was converted to oil. Elsewhere under the building, the crawlspace averaged two feet in height. That meant we had to climb up from the corridor into the areas under investigation, and then crawl back into the site with flood lamps and work lying on our stomachs or sides.

The dirt was so fine that the slightest disturbance resulted in clouds of choking dust. We could not trowel or sift, so we set the vacuum cleaner in the corridor. We covered the hose end with fine one-fourth inch wire screen to ensure no bones, teeth, or artifacts were sucked away during excavation. We also used respirator masks. The area we chose to investigate was in a different cellar than the ossuary. It was almost directly in front of the sealed door. We arduously drove planks shoring down into the ground, forming a square. That created an essentially buried box. We could then excavate what was within the box while the boards held back loose sand. The first test pit we dug in this manner proved to be empty. We then put in a second pit, which abutted the first's west side. When we came to the bottom of this pit, we found that a shoring plank on the west side pierced the foot of a sealed wooden coffin. We formed an area eight feet long and three feet wide by driving down more shoring. We then excavated down to the coffin, finally exposing the body. Unlike the ossuary bones, these bones were in a state of extreme decomposition. Little remained but feet and leg bones. The hips and spine were little more than a calcium line in the bottom of the box. All that remained of the head was some teeth and hair tied with a piece of rawhide.

The degree of decomposition we found here was due to two factors. First, the body was buried inside a coffin. Second, the extremely fine soil created a nearly airtight seal around it. This resulted in moisture retention in and around the body, therefore, much more decay of the skeleton. The ossuary bodies, on the other hand, having been buried out-of-doors without coffins or church buildings to protect them, quickly lost all their tissue. Once the flesh was gone, the bones could last almost indefinitely.

We felt it might be possible to determine the identity of one or more of the legitimate burials because it was the practice to put an individual's name on his or her coffin. A wood fragment from the collapsed lid of the excavated coffin revealed the letters S and R formed by iron tacks. From the study of the church and court records, we found a Samuel Roades, twelve years old. A later examination of the teeth by Dr. Stanley Schwartz, forensic dental examiner for the Commonwealth of Massachusetts, confirmed they belong to a twelve-year-old. Dr. Schwartz also examined the teeth of the skulls I had at Codman House and provided each skull's approximate age.

We were finally able to locate the ten recorded burials that lie roughly in a row at a depth of three feet and to the west of the now filled-in corridor. We were also able to establish them as separate and distinct from those at the ossuary location.

St. Michael's Church was built in 1714 in what Marblehead, Massachusetts. is now. It was an Anglican mission outpost in the Puritan bastion of New England. It is somewhat ironic since one of the major reasons the Puritans emigrated to New England was to establish their own theocracy, free from the dominance of the Anglican Church.

Anti-Anglican feeling ran high in the colony. St. Michael's was established in this hostile setting to minister to the small minority of Anglicans and to serve in a missionary capacity to win back Puritan dissenters to the Anglican Church, today known as the Episcopalian Church.

An examination of church records revealed the following ten people as those in the legitimate burials.

1715
- John Horton, two days old
- Byrd, four years old
- Jane Redd, adult
- Mary Tyler, adult
- Samuel Roades, twelve years old
- Mary Goodwin, eleven years old

1716
- Samuel Redd, adult
- Tamsond Kane, age unknown
- Mary Gatchell, three years old
- James Bird, one year old

We worked at night and slept during the day on the parish house floor, surviving on peanut butter sandwiches. The excavation then began to progress on a regular schedule and revealed significant findings.

We were able to expose the original church's ground surface, which was covered with layers of ash, charcoal, and plaster. The mixture also included red plaster from 1833 when the altar was moved. Together, these formed a very distinct stratigraphic unit that varied in thickness from one side to another. It started at seven centimeters and reached eleven centimeters before thinning again as it neared the northern wall of the basement.

The ossuary was located under the altar during the first century of the church's existence. This precise location was clearly intended to give the bones the most sacred place under the Church. Bringing the bones to the basement indicated affection and respect. The location was also a clue about the people involved in the internment.

Stephen and I carefully removed all the disturbed soil and exposed the bones still lying-in situ. We found six more skulls, bringing the total to seventeen individuals. Every bone or tooth we found was moved to the Codman House.

We then mapped, photographed, and recorded the different features and their association to one another. In addition, we found some black painted planks that were probably parts of the coffins used to transport the bodies. Those planks also suggested the area where they buried the bones.

Reading books and documents related to the Salem trials and hangings; I learned those seventeen people were buried in common graves. The other three victims were retrieved by their families and buried in undisclosed locations.

Since they were convicted as witches and considered criminals, they were forever denied a Christian burial. Officials at the time passed a law forbidding disinterring the bodies. It was punishable by death.

Everything fell in place. Even Stephen, who was skeptical initially, was finally convinced that the remains belonged to Salem's executions. Before he left, he produced a map of the basement of the church, with the location of the legitimate burials, the ossuary, doors, corridors, and furnace.

After a few weeks, Stephen had to return to his studies, and I also had my jobs. I continued the excavation alone, at a much slower pace, until I had the certainty that the ossuary pit was thoroughly examined, and no more human vestiges were left undiscovered. It took more than one year to accomplish that goal and recover every single bone.

It is difficult to describe how uncomfortable and exhausting the excavation was. The basement was extremely cold, a very narrow space in which to move and turn, and the fine dust that, even with a respiratory mask, clung to the clothes and hair and found its way to the lungs. Still, I was determined to keep looking for one more tooth or tiny bone that could add more clues for the identification of the victims.

The next step was to obtain the study and opinion of professional forensic specialists to identify the bodies and estimate their age and sex. If they corresponded to the ones executed, I would have the certainty that my theory was correct.

For that purpose, I contacted Dr. Neil Gomberg, PH.D., University of Massachusetts. Professor of Physical Anthropology at Brandeis University, Dr. Dena Ferran Dincauze Ph.D., Harvard University; Professor of Archaeology at the University of Massachusetts, and Dr. Stanley Schwartz, DMU U Mass Ph. D. Anthropology, Doctor for the Commonwealth of Massachusetts in Forensic Medicine Dentistry.

There were no funds for this project, so they worked for free, through weekends and in their spare time. The magnitude of the findings was enough reward for them. They were willing to contribute to that part of American history. They needed almost one year to complete their study.

It was always conducted in total secrecy until the connection to Salem Trials would be beyond doubt and the results could be of public knowledge.

They stated that most of the small bones—ribs, vertebrae, and teeth, and the bones of the hands and feet—were missing. The bones were completely disarticulated and mixed in a way that would have been impossible if there had been flesh attached to them. That corroborated the secondary burial assessment.

Dr. Schwartz observed several fractured axial and radial vertebrae. These are the first two vertebrae below the neck. According to his observation, this condition would be caused by a sudden snapping movement, such as could be expected from hanging.

Dr. Dincauze and Dr. Schwartz agreed that the teeth indicated an early European colonial population. Contributing evidence included nutritional deficiency, excessive wear, a high number of cavities, loss of teeth, and other dental abnormalities. The damage started in early adulthood. It didn't provide much information about the individual's exact age but certainly belonged to the same period and life conditions.

By then, there were seventeen planks with their corresponding skulls. Gomberg, Dincauze, and Schwartz matched what they considered could be the hips and legs of the same age and sex of each skull. The conclusions of their study were as follows.

- Four skulls could not be identified because of extensive damage or deterioration.
- Of the identified skulls, five were male and eight were female.
- There were seventeen bodies in total.
- Twenty people were executed by the following methods at the Salem trials.
  - **Hanging**
    - Five males
    - Fourteen females
  - **Crushing**
    - One male

In order to obtain a confession, the crushing victim was tortured using pressure on the chest in the form of stones and bricks. Ultimately, the victim's ribs collapsed and punctured the lungs, and he stopped breathing.

The identification of the bones considered the age and sex based on the characteristics of the skulls, teeth, hips, and vertebrae. The level of arthritis and osteoporosis were good indications of age.

The skulls were then identified by Dr. Neil Gomberg.

He found the birthdate[s] of the executed victims. Comparing those dates with the ages of the skulls, he came out with this list, but it is mostly guest work because of the damage to many of the bones, probably produced with the tools used to disinter them.

Some of the skulls had too much damage, so it was difficult to determine if they were male or female. Since five males were interred, he decided to start with the five definite male skulls and assigned [each] a name according to the approximate age.

Males
- John Willard, age 35, executed August 19, 1692 (approximate age 30s)
- Wilmott Reed, age 54, executed September 22, 1962 (approximate age 50s)
- John Proctor, age 60, executed August 19, 1962 (approximate age 55)
- Samuel Wardwell, age 47 executed September 22, 1692 (approximate age over 30)
- George Burroughs, age 42, executed August 19, 1692 (approximate age 40s). Burroughs's physique was described as "puny." The sawn skull recovered was relatively small and of the correct age of Burroughs.

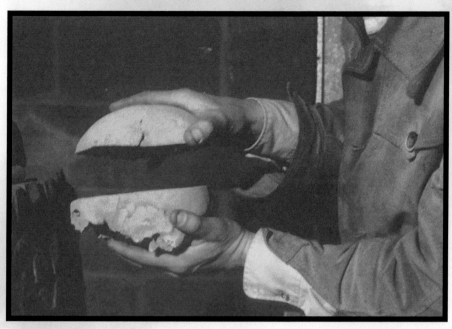

(Sawn skull)

Females

- Bridget Bishop, age 32, executed June 10, 1692 (she was the first; approximate age 25)
- Sarah Good, age 38, executed July 19, 1692 (approximate age 20s–30s)
- Elizabeth Howe, age 57, executed July 19, 1692 (approximate age 40s–-50s)
- Susannah Martin, age 71, executed July 19, 1692(approximate age over 50)
- Sara Wildes, age 65, executed July 19, 1692(approximate age over 50)
- Martha Carrier, age 42, executed August 19, 1692 (approximate age 30s)
- Martha Corey, age 72, executed September 22, 1692 (approximate age over 50)
- Mary Eastey, age 58, executed September 22, 1692 (approximate age over 50)
- Mary Parker, age 61, executed September 22, 1692 (approximate age over 30)
- Alice Parker, age 58, executed September 22, 1692 (approximate age 50s)
- Ann Pudeator, age 70, executed September 1692 (approximate age over 50)
- Margaret Scott, age 77, executed September 22, 1692 (approximate age 50)

Only DNA tests will provide more accurate ages of the skulls, but in general the ages of the skulls and the executed victims were similar enough to assume that they were the executed victims.

Bodies taken by their families after hanging

- Rebecca Nurse, age 71, executed July 19, 1692
- George Jacobs, age 83, executed August 19, 1692

(Thirteen skulls)

Additional information was gathered from the sawn skull. Horizontal knife cuts, plainly visible on the sides of the cranium, show where the scalp was removed. This was necessary to keep the fine teeth of the saw from binding. The frontal bone had also been cut through to expose the sinus cavities.

After the opinions and conclusions from Dr. Schwartz, Dr. Dincauze, and Dr Gomberg were considered final, the work was finished. We had no doubts that the bones belonged to the Salem Trials victims.

It took almost two years.

My last job was returning the remains to their resting place. I carefully placed them in small boxes and took them back to the basement of St. Michael's church.

By August 1980, all the bones were in place. I closed the door and never came back.

(Five skulls, almost toothless)

(Ten skulls at the basement)

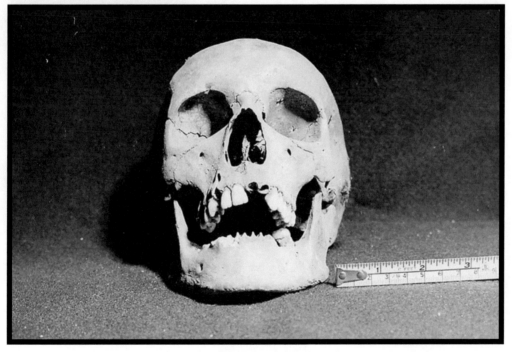

(Skull close-up)

(Vertebrae)

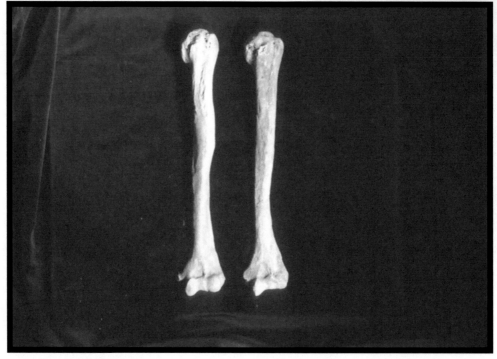

(Two femur bones)

(Skull close up damaged)

(Skull, toothless, up close)

(Small blackboard with date and location at the basement)

(Assorted bones and small blackboard with date and location)

(Curtis Chapin with respiratory mask, in the basement using the vacuum)

(Curtis Chapin, classifying bones in the basement)

(Skulls in the basement, close up)

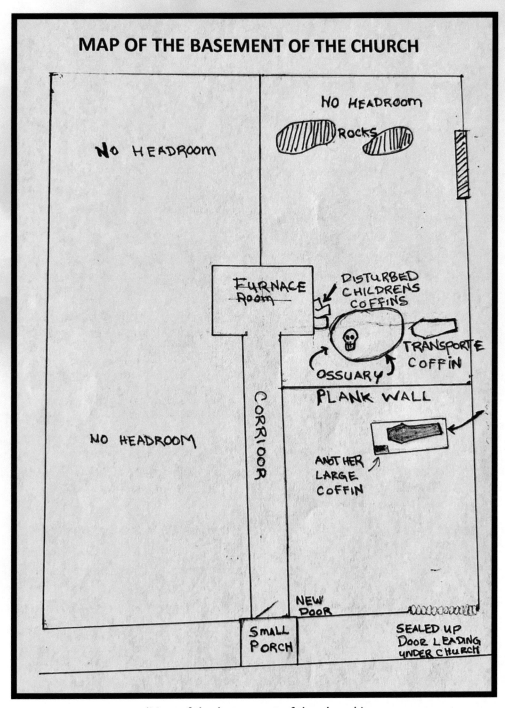

(Map of the basement of the church)

CHAPTER 2

Then

Several factors contributed to start the witch-hunt in Salem and the neighboring villages.

Between the fifteenth and nineteenth centuries, the Northern Hemisphere went through a period of colder temperatures, identified in 1940 as the Little Ice Age. The cold was not constant, and it worsened during certain periods. The end of the seventeenth century was one of them. The winters were colder and summers warmer than usual. In Europe, witch-hunts intensified, and they reached the colonies during the first century of their existence.

The bitter cold forced farmers to stay, more than usual, indoors. Sadness and boredom increased. The daylight hours were barely seven. Youngsters were susceptible to feeling scared and threatened by their own shadows. The source of light during the long dark hours was scarce: the chimney, some candles and oil lamps.

At the Reverend Samuel Parris's home, there was also bitterness. His fee payments were delayed and the amount of wood that was stipulated in his contract was not delivered as promised. His daughters were listening to their parents' complaints and gossip.

The presence of the devil was real for everybody. Church sermons reminded parishioners of the presence of Satan among them. The devil's works were responsible for damaged crops, stillborn babies, dead animals, and the increased number of illnesses. Common sense was overpowered by the belief in supernatural powers.

At Reverend Parris's home, two girls—his daughter Betty Parris, age nine, and his niece Abigail Williams, age eleven, started suffering strange and scary symptoms: seizures, paralysis, and screaming. The doctor was unable to diagnose much less heal them. His opinion was that a witch's power produced the torments. When interrogated further, the girls accused the slave Tituba of bewitching them.

Reverend Parris brought Tituba with him when he came from Barbados, where he had ministered for a few years. It is not clear if she was of Indian or African descent, but she had dark skin. Santeria was the common belief throughout the Caribbean islands. They believe in the power of prayer to saints and the use of herbs for different purposes, either for good or bad intentions. Santeria came from Africa to Cuba with the black slaves and was rapidly adopted by the islanders. It is still very popular in Latin countries and even in the present United States. More than five million people are believers. Since Santeria involves the worship of saints, it could have been an adaptation of the Catholicism brought by missionaries to Africa. That included the figure of Satan as the fallen angel.

For the African converts, who used to worship the sun, the rain, and natural events, to praise the human figures of saints was far more comprehensible than an invisible God. They could identify much easier with them. They were the shortcut to draw God's attention to their prayers and needs. Witch doctors used herbs and other substances to produce potions for healing illnesses and granting wishes. Throughout time, those beliefs and practices were considered magic, either white or black. Associated with Satan, witchcraft become a threat to the Church, and witches were prosecuted and killed.

Tituba, confessed at the trials to practice witchcraft, from Barbados she probably brought the beliefs and rituals of Santeria and to entertain the girls during the long hours of darkness and shadows, easily terrified the girls with stories of apparitions and evil spirits. The girls were young, bored, and sensitive. When the girls accused Tituba of bewitching them, she admitted having witch powers.

Under pressure, the girls also accused two women who, they had learned from the gossip among adults, were undesirable and annoying. Despised by everybody in town, their guilt was immediately accepted. Ann Putnam and Rebecca Nurse were accused and jailed. The spark ignited a fire.

The girls were suddenly popular and pitied for their suffering. Other girls followed. They became the accusers and the accused mostly old women.

Envy, old grudges, and uncommon or sinful behavior were among the hidden motives for accusation. The girls sometimes did not know the people they accused. They just heard the names from the adults, and gossip became a deadly weapon. Church sermons only added more fear of the devil's presence and power.

The accusation of Reverend George Burroughs increased the number of accusations. If a minister started worshiping the devil and being controlled by him, nobody was safe. Satan was everywhere. The fear and hysteria spread to neighboring towns like Danvers, Andover, Ipswich, Beverly, Boston, and others.

The judges agreed to accept "specter"—the vision of a ghost—as evidence and proof of witchcraft. That irrational decision made the accusations unstoppable. One hundred fifty people were imprisoned and accused. The conditions of the jail were unhealthy, cold, and sickening. Some died in prison.

In Europe and in other parts of the United States, accused witches were burnt or hanged independently of their confessions. In Salem, a confession was necessary to confirm the guilt and execution. Giles Corey was pressed to death to obtain his confession.

In Salem, the accused who confessed to being witches were set free. They were considered innocent because they belonged to Satan, and they were able to continue with their lives undisturbed. They confessed to avoid death. A confessed witch, Tituba, was acquitted.

Who cut Burroughs's skull? Cotton Mather was very interested in the brains of criminals; he considered them different from the brains of normal and good people. He wrote books on the subject without the benefit of forensic evidence. How could he compare? Autopsies were forbidden.

The accused who refused to confess, to pledge their unmovable faith in Christ, and to believe in eternal salvation and access to paradise were executed. Burroughs was saying the Lord's Prayer with the noose around his neck.

Another situation not mentioned at the trials also became a matter for suspicion among the people.

The first arrivals to America were followers of the Puritan faith. They left England to avoid the rejection of the Anglicans, the majority religious group, who they thought were too close to the Catholic Church. Anglican believers eventually arrived in the colonies. They tried to blend in with the established community but were still thought of as old enemies.

Phillip English, for example, was an Anglican originally from England. He sometimes allowed services to be held at his home. He and his wife were accused and jailed in Salem but escaped to New York before the hangings started. English later became an ardent critic of the judges, the trial procedures, and the executions. Many years later, he obtained some reimbursement for the families of the victims. His efforts continued, and in future settlements, all the martyrs' descendants received some level of compensation and complete recognition of their innocence. Their deaths, however, were beyond innocence designation. They understood refusing to believe in Satan and maintaining their absolute and unbending belief in God would become a death sentence, and Heaven was the final recompense. The certainty of Paradise was more powerful than the fear of torture and death. Martyrdom was their choice.

It is impossible to confirm how many of the victims were Anglican and if the proceedings represented an attempt at religious vengeance. Burroughs was a Puritan minister. Probably some Anglican believers turned to the Puritan church to avoid confrontations and blend into the community.

This new approach to the Trials maybe will generate further investigations to find the true beliefs of the martyrs.

(Memorial bench at Salem, Massachusetts)

A monument engraved with the names of the victims was built in Salem.

CHAPTER 3

A Theory

Curtis had a theory that was impossible for him to prove. He believed the trials and murders were perpetrated as religiously motivated revenge. Were all the martyrs Anglicans? Why did they all end up under an Anglican church? The only way to prove his theory involved finding the baptismal certificate of each one of the victims. If they came from England, the registration would be there. That investigation was beyond his resources and health. However, it is a project for future investigations.

The mystery was there and based on some findings he developed a theory. How did seventeen bodies get from Salem to Marblehead? It must have been a well-planned scheme. Several difficulties were involved for all the conspirators. The death penalty had been established for anybody who removed one or more bodies from their graves. It was a capital offense. Secrecy, resources, and the locations of four different burial sites were among the most difficult obstacles.

There were four different grave locations. Since the hangings happened during the summer, one month apart, the option of using the same grave was impossible since the smell of the decaying bodies would have been unbearable. They needed the assistance of a reliable witness for all four executions. Who would have had the information, courage, means, and decision to execute the plan? According to history, two figures had the profile to do so. One was pivotal. William Piggott was rector of St. Michael's Church, an Anglican haven in the middle of an authoritarian and unforgiving Puritan majority. The Anglican church was built in 1714, twenty-two years after the executions.

Piggott knew from the start, the details of the church's construction, the rooms, corridors, basement, beams, and materials used. He had all the necessary information about the underground layout and the location of the door that led to that level, which was sealed some years later. He also approved the interment of ten parishioners between 1715 and 1716. Was this a prelude to the future reburial of Salem martyrs? And where there only ten? Maybe since the construction of the Church he created the underground space just big enough for some parishioner's coffins and the boxes with the Salem victims. The ten recorded burials made the basement an official cemetery. Sacred ground.

The second suspect Curtis thought was involved in the project, was Phillip English. He made his life mission to obtain justice for the victims. He was a deacon of the church, made donations for the construction, and was a close friend of Piggott. He was a rich man, owner of many seagoing vessels and loyal employees. He had been an admired Anglican leader and very religious. Born in 1651, English was approaching his seventies and could not waste any time. He needed some loyal and strong men.

Neither English nor Piggott witnessed the executions. Therefore, they must have needed informants in order to keep up with the events. These informants could have been the same family members who witnessed the hangings and would have known the exact location of the graves. One grave had one body, Bridget Bishop, a woman executed on June 10. On July 19, five people were hanged: Sarah Good, Elizabeth Howe, Susannah Martin, Sara Wildes, and Rebecca Nurse. Rebecca Nurse's body was rescued by her family and taken to an unknown location. The one grave dug on August 19 had four bodies: Martha Carrier and three men, John Willard, John Proctor, and George Burroughs. George Jacobs was also executed that day, but his body was recovered by his family. Recently, in a farm that used to belong to the Jacobs family, some bones were found. September 22 was the bloodiest execution date as eight people died, Martha Corey, Mary Eastey, Mary Parker, Alice Parker, Ann Pudeator, Margaret Scott, Wilmott Reed, and Samuel Wardwell. Witnesses in the area stated that the pits were not deep enough as the bodies were not thoroughly covered with soil. There were instances where bones would be visible above ground. Family members placed discreet marks the next days to remember the untouchable graves.

Returning to English, he still had friends and colleagues living in Salem. After twenty-two years, he could find a witness to point out the location of the four graves. The search for them had to be done at night, and a full moon was necessary since lanterns would draw too much attention from neighbors and dogs. Dark clothes, gloves, hoods, and faces darkened with coal dust were also required. He built two boxes painted in black; these are the same boxes Curtis found under the church. Considering that a full moon was needed to see and avoid suspicion, Curtis presumed that it was done during the autumn Harvest Moon. At that time, frozen soil was not an issue, and neither were the warmer temperatures that encouraged people to remain outdoors during the night. The full moon makes the dogs bark and howl, and this noise wouldn't attract attention. Next step in the journey would have been to cross the river, therefore two wooden crafts were brought to shore near Proctor Ledge, with English leading the operation and some trustworthy helpers. Once the group met the informants/witnesses they would be led to the graves. Due to the missing bones retrieved on this century we can assume the following. Picking up the remains was an extremely difficult task to perform under the low light and arduous circumstances. They had to use their hands to separate the bones from the stones, small bones were easily confused with gravel; ribs could be mistaken with roots and branches. They missed most of them. They also used tools that damaged most of the skulls even those from June's grave when it only held one corpse. July, August, and September graves were more challenging and messier to retrieve. The flesh was gone, and a pile of skeletons would have been impossible to separate or identify. They only had between six to eight hours under the moonlight to finish the work.

After they counted seventeen skulls, including the two halves of George Burroughs's skull (which probably puzzled them), they considered the work done. All the bones went inside the black boxes, but now they weren't just boxes, they were coffins. Before leaving, they refilled the pits, smoothed the soil, and covered it with stones and branches, trying to leave no trace. There was no chance for a second expedition. Their lives were at stake. They rowed across the river, reaching Marblehead shore perhaps as the first light peaked the silhouette of the church tower. They walked uphill cautiously, avoiding the watchmen of the night. They brought the coffins through the small door, and carefully placed them side by side, under the altar, providing a blessed shelter to the seventeen victims. Now they could rest in peace. Father Piggott offered a prayer for their souls, and the first martyrs of North America found their secret resting place on sacred soil.

It was Curtis' theory that only a profound religious belief could had driven them to perform such a difficult and life-threatening project.

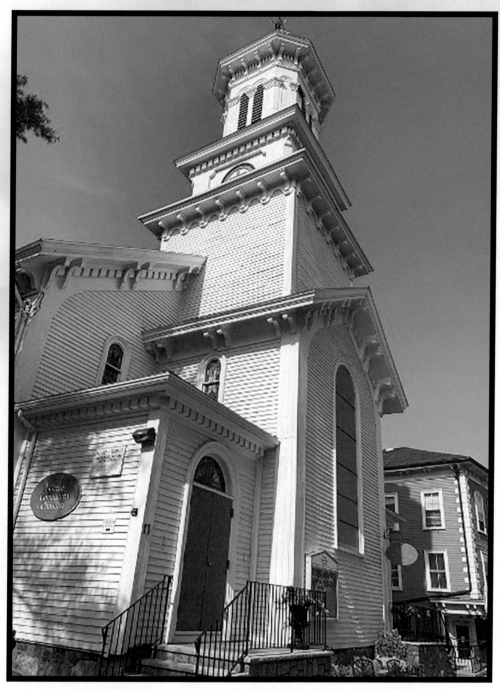

(St. Michael's Church, Marblehead, Massachusetts)

(Plaque on the side wall of St. Michael's Church, Marblehead, Massachusetts)

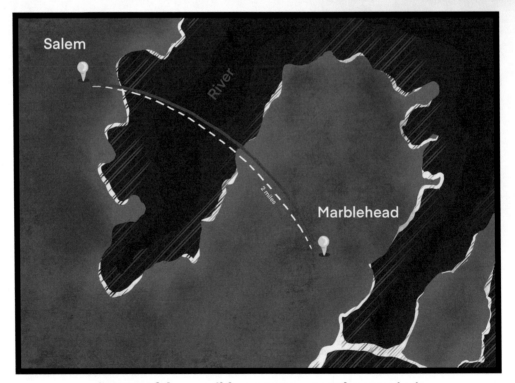

(Image of the possible route to move the remains)

REFERENCES

These books were in Curtis's library.

Adams, James Truslow. *The Founding of New England*. Boston, MA: Atlantic Monthly Press, 1949.

Bailyn, Bernard. *The New England Merchants in the Seventeenth Century*. Cambridge, MA: Harvard University Press, 1955.

Baker, Emerson W. *A Storm of Witchcraft*. Oxford, UK: Oxford University Press, 2015.

Boyer, Paul, and Stephen Nissenbaum. *Salem Possessed: The Social Origins of Witchcraft*. Cambridge, MA: Harvard University Press, 1974.

Cooke, William H. *Justice at Salem*. Revised ed. South Carolina: Create Space Publishing, 2014

Cummings, Abbott Lowell. *Rural Household Inventories: Establishing the Names, Uses and Furnishings of Rooms in the Colonial New England Home 1675-1775*. Portland, ME: Anthoensen Press, 1964.

Hansen, Chadwick. *Witchcraft at Salem*. New York: George Braziller, 1969.

Hill, Frances. *A Delusion of Satan: The Full Story of the Salem Witch Trials*. Cambridge, MA: Da Capo Press, 1995

Hytner, Nicholas, dir. *The Crucible*. United States: Twentieth Century Fox, 1996.

Miller, Perry, and Thomas H. Johnson, eds. *The Puritans*. Vol. 1. New York, NY: Harper Torchbooks, 1963.

Nevins, Winfield S. *Witchcraft in Salem Village in 1692, Together with a Review of the Opinions of Modern Writers and Psychologists in Regard to Outbreak of the Evil in America*. 5th ed. New York, NY: Lenox Hill Press, 1971.

Norton, Mary Beth. *In the Devil's Snare: The Salem Witchcraft Crisis of 1692*. New York, NY: Vintage, 2003.

Roach, Marilynne K. *The Salem Witch Trials: A Day-by-Day Chronicle of a Community Under Seige*. Lanham, MD: Cooper Square Press, 2002.

———. *Six Women of Salem: The Untold Story of the Accused and Their Accusers in the Salem Witch Trials*. Philadelphia, PA: Da Capo Press, 2013.

Rosenthal, Bernard, ed. *Records of the Salem Witch-Hunt*. Cambridge, UK: Cambridge University Press, 2012

Schiff, Stacy. *The Witches: Suspicion, Betrayal, and Hysteria in 1692 Salem*. New York, NY: Back Bay Books, 2015.

Schneider, Herbert Wallace. *The Puritan Mind*. New York, NY: Henry Holt and Company, 1961.

Upham, Charles W. *Salem Witchcraft, Volumes I and II*. New York, NY: Frederick Ungar, 1978.

Wright, John Hardy. *Sorcery in Salem (Images of America: Massachusetts)*. Portsmouth, NH: Arcadia Publishing, 1999

Williams, Charles. *Witchcraft*. London, UK: Faber and Faber, 1941.

ACKNOWLEGMENTS

Robert Howie, St. Michael's archivist, Marblehead, Massachusetts

Dr. Stephen Loring, Ph.D., University of Massachusetts; Anthropology Assistant to the Chairman of the Smithsonian Institution, Department of Anthropology/Artic Archaeologist, National Museum of Natural History

Dr. Neil Gomberg, Ph.D., University of Massachusetts; Professor of Physical Anthropology at Brandeis University

Dr. Dena Dincauze, Ph.D., Harvard University; Professor of Archaeology at the University of Massachusetts

Dr. Stanley Schwartz, DMD U Mass PhD Anthropology; Doctor for the Commonwealth of Massachusetts in Forensic Medicine Dentistry

Printed in the United States
by Baker & Taylor Publisher Services